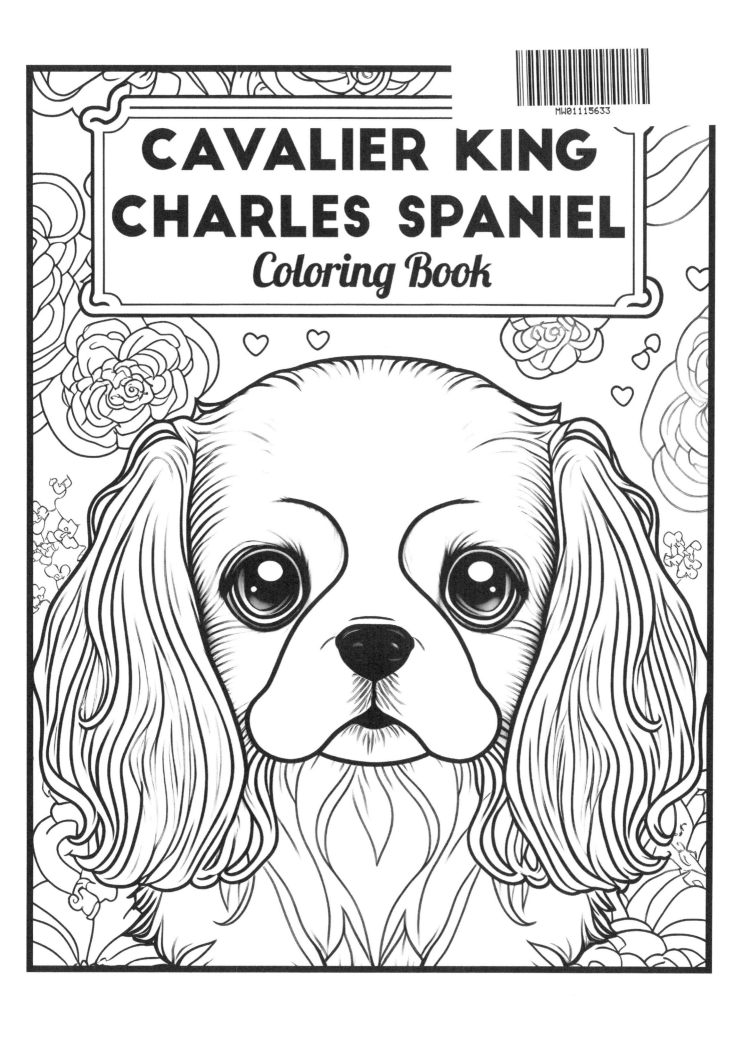

Made in the USA
Middletown, DE
09 September 2024

60570536R00051

The Wealth
Connect

The Wealth Connect

Your Pathway to Financial Freedom

Shareef "Ross Mac" McDonald

MACONOMIC$

PUBLISHED BY MACONOMICS LLC

Maconomics books may be purchased for educational, business or sales promotional use. For information visit Maconomics.com.

Publishing Consultant: JinJa Birkenbeuel, Birk Creative
Designed by JinJa Birkenbeuel, Birk Creative
Illustrations by Fenton Shaw

Printed in the United States of America
Published by Maconomics LLC
ISBN 979-8-9885919-1-7

Gratitude shapes this journey, and there are treasured individuals whose support and love have been instrumental.

To my parents, who instilled in me a relentless drive and the essence of resilience, your sacrifices are the foundation of my achievements.

To my wife, my beacon of light, your unwavering support and faith have fueled my ambitions. You are my sanctuary and strength.

My children, you are my inspiration, purpose, and the embodiment of a better future. Every word I write is for your world.

To my family, your enduring love and support remind me that I am not alone. Your strength bolsters me in every endeavor.

And to my mentors, your wisdom and guidance have honed my leadership and perspective. Your challenges have fostered my continuous growth.

This work is dedicated to all of you. Thank you for being an integral part of my journey, shaping me into the man and leader I am today.

Table of Contents

"Don't give your kids everything you didn't have growing

up, instead, teach them everything you didn't know."

Ross Mac

Chapter One

The Power of Budgeting: The Cornerstone of Generational Wealth

There are no shortcuts to building wealth in the pursuit of changing your family's trajectory. Contrary to popular belief, financial success doesn't come from a stroke of luck, an inheritance or having a high revenue job. It begins with understanding the value of every dollar you earn and how to allocate it effectively to accumulate wealth. In order to truly build wealth, you have to change your relationship with money and allow money to be a tool rather than a means to an end. Money is a tool when used properly.

If you're reading this book, you are being intentional about building generational wealth and securing financial freedom for yourself and the generations to come. Being intentional starts with understanding your inflows and outflows to better align with your financial goals. How do you do that? Budgeting.

At its core, budgeting is a financial plan that outlines your income and expenditures over a given period. It provides you with a roadmap of your financial health, allowing you to track your income, manage your expenses, and prioritize your savings and investments. This is the first pivotal step to financial planning as it plays an indispensable role in achieving financial freedom.

> "Wealth is the ability to fully experience life."
> **Henry David Thoreau**

Budgeting helps ensure you aren't living beyond your means. Without a budget, it's easy to spend money carelessly, where you often end up in a constant cycle of living paycheck to paycheck. A well-planned budget ensures that your expenses do not exceed your income, safeguarding you from falling into debt or relying on credit to meet your basic needs.

Budgeting isn't merely about restricting your spending; it's about creating space to save and invest. With a budget, you can allocate a portion of your income towards savings and investments, which is the only way to build generational wealth. If you are in debt, a budget is a powerful tool that can help you manage and eventually overcome it. By allocating funds to debt repayment, you'll see your debts reducing gradually until they're fully paid off.

The holy grail and most recommended budgeting tool you can use to manage your finances is the 50/30/20 rule. The rule suggests dividing your after-tax income in the following way:

50% on Needs: Half of your income should go towards your needs, such as housing, food, health care, and other essential bills. These are the things you need in order to function and survive.

30% on Wants: Thirty percent of your income can be allocated to wants - the things you enjoy but could live without if necessary, like entertainment, eating out, and hobbies.

20% on Savings, Debt Payments and Investing: The remaining twenty percent should be allocated towards saving, paying down debt and investing. Once you have attacked your debt, the vast majority of this allocation will go toward investing.

To apply the 50/30/20 rule to get out of debt, start by listing all your monthly expenses and categorizing them into needs, wants, and savings/debt payments. Once you've categorized and tallied up each category, calculate what percentage of your income each category represents.

If after taxes, you make $5,000 per month, your rent should not be $2,500. Why? Because rent alone is 50% of your income and you still haven't accounted for groceries, utility bill or insurance.

Being intentional starts with visualizing where you are financially so that you can prioritize where you need to cut back in certain areas to reach your goals.

"You don't have to see the whole staircase, just take the first step."
Martin Luther King, Jr.

Chapter Two

The Path to Freedom: Escaping the Chains of Debt

The hardest road to travel along the path of achieving financial freedom is undoubtedly overcoming debt. This is the perpetual hamster wheel that has become so common that people often find it easier to keep going rather than getting off the wheel. However, you are not alone! According to the Federal Reserve Bank of New York's Household Debt and Credit report, the average American has over $50K in debt. But now is the time to become intentional about breaking the cycle.

Debt, in its simplest terms, is money borrowed that must be repaid, often with interest. While strategic borrowing can sometimes be a tool for financial growth, such as a mortgage for a home or a loan for a profitable business, debt often serves as a weight that drags down your financial wellbeing. The interest that accumulates over time can stifle your ability to save, invest, and ultimately build wealth.

Escaping debt is not just about lifting the weight off your finances it's about reclaiming your financial freedom. It reduces interest payments, and when you weigh in high interest bearing credit cards, this is money that should instead go towards wealth building activities. By eliminating debt, you free up income that can be invested and you substantially lower stress factors.

Living in constant debt is in fact stealing from your future self. That's why formalizing an actionable plan

> "Debt is the new American slavery, and its chains are made of credit cards."
> **Elizabeth Warren**

to tackle debt once and for all is a priority. A recommended strategy for you to adapt is the Debt Snowball Method.

The Debt Snowball Method is a debt reduction strategy where you pay off debts in order of smallest to largest, gaining momentum as each balance is paid off. Here's how it works:

1. Start by listing all your debts, excluding your mortgage, from smallest to largest regardless of the interest rate.
2. Make minimum payments on all your debts except the smallest.
3. Pay as much as possible on your smallest debt. Once that debt is gone, take its payment and apply it to the next smallest debt.
4. Continue the process until each debt is paid in full. As the payments roll over from one debt to the next, it creates a 'snowball effect', enabling you to pay off larger debts faster.

It's important to note that the Debt Snowball Method is not the fastest or least expensive method of debt repayment (that would be the Debt Avalanche Method, which prioritizes debts with the highest interest rates), but it can provide psychological wins that boost motivation, a crucial factor in the often challenging journey to debt freedom.

In the subsequent chapters, we will delve into other key aspects of building generational wealth, such as establishing an emergency fund and investing. Remember, debt elimination is not just about getting rid of loans; it's about reclaiming your income and freeing yourself to pursue your financial goals unimpeded.

"What I really wanted to do is just transform inner city kids all around the world to start having a conversation like, 'What's a better company, Microsoft or Apple? The way they compare LeBron to Jordan."
Ross Mac

"You must gain control over your money or the lack

of it will forever control you."

Dave Ramsey

Chapter Three

The Safety Net: Building Your Emergency Fund

As we continue on our path to establishing generational wealth, it's important to discuss the role of an emergency fund in your financial journey. After mastering the art of budgeting and creating a strategy to escape debt, the next vital step is to establish an emergency fund.

An emergency fund is a stash of money set aside to cover the financial surprises life throws your way. These unexpected events can be anything from an out-of-pocket medical expense, an unanticipated car repair, a sudden job loss, or any other expense that isn't part of your regular budget.

An emergency fund is not just crucial, but it's indispensable to your financial health and the journey towards building generational wealth. It provides you with a sense of financial security knowing you have resources available to cushion financial blows without resorting to credit or loans, which can potentially thrust you back into debt. Using credit cards for emergencies is a recipe for disaster.

Having an emergency fund can grant you the freedom to make life choices without the constant fear of financial instability. For example, it can provide the financial cushion needed to switch jobs or careers, or to weather a period of unemployment.

Financial concerns stand as one of the primary drivers of stress for many individuals. Having an emergency fund can greatly reduce your financial anxiety knowing you're prepared for unexpected expenses. Without an emergency fund, you may be forced to dip into your investments or savings in times of financial need, thereby interrupting the compounding growth of your wealth, or even worse, resorting to taking out loans.

So how much should you have in your emergency fund and where should you put it?

A rule of thumb suggested by most financial experts is to aim for three to six months worth of necessary living expenses. This may seem like a daunting task at first, but remember, you don't need to fund it overnight. Start small and increase your contributions over time. This is where your budgeting skills will come into play, ensuring you allocate a portion of your income to your emergency fund consistently.

To determine if you need closer to three or six months worth of your necessary expenses is predicated on where you are in your life. If you don't possess a high level of job security, it's recommended to get closer to six. If you have children, it's also recommended you have closer to six. The way this math works is using your budget template. If your necessary expenses sums to $2,000, and you have children, you should have $12,000 saved in your emergency fund.

Now that we understand the amount, let's discuss where you should keep your emergency fund.

Your emergency fund should be easily accessible, but not so accessible that you're tempted to dip into it for non-emergencies. Consider keeping it in a high-yield savings account, where it can earn a higher amount of interest than traditional checking/savings accounts, but can be accessed quickly when needed.

Building an emergency fund is a fundamental step towards financial independence and security. While it may not directly contribute to generating wealth, it protects your financial foundation, ensuring that when life's storms come - and they will - you're ready to weather them without crippling your financial future.

In the chapters to come, we will explore the power of investing and delve into strategies for wealth accumulation. Just as a house needs a strong foundation before it can be built, your financial house needs a solid base - and an emergency fund is a critical part of that base.

> "He who buys what he does not need, steals from himself."
> **Swedish Proverb**

Chapter Four

The Silent Killer: Why You NEED To Invest

Having established the importance of budgeting, debt elimination, and the creation of an emergency fund, we now move to a crucial aspect of wealth creation - investing. Investing, particularly in the stock market, is one of the most effective ways to build wealth over the long term. This chapter will explain why it's virtually impossible to save your way to wealth and how investing helps you stay ahead of inflation.

There's a common misconception that saving money is the same as growing wealth. We all have heard our parents or grandparents say, "make sure you save your money." While saving, particularly in an emergency fund, is an essential part of financial security, it's not a strategy for wealth generation.

On average, traditional savings accounts offer annual returns of about 0.33%. This generates 33 cents for every hundred dollars in your savings account, which means your money truly isn't working for you. It's sitting in a bank, generating a return that isn't keeping pace with inflation. Banks take in your deposits, pay very little interest on those deposits, and then lend that money out to individuals or businesses at a much higher interest rate, pocketing the difference. The small interest the banks pay you isn't enough. Why? Because your money is losing its value.

Inflation is the rate at which the general level of prices for goods and services are rising, and subsequently, purchasing power is falling. Inflation is the silent killer of wealth. When your grandparents were younger, they could brag about how gasoline cost them less than $1 and a cart full of groceries was less than $5. Clearly that isn't the case anymore!

As inflation rises, the value of your money diminishes because your dollars can't buy as much as they once used to. This is why investing becomes critical. At a bare minimum, the goal should be to invest so that your money outpaces the rate of inflation. The average rate of inflation in the U.S. is roughly 2-3% annually. Meaning that if you had $100 a year ago, that would only be worth roughly $97-$98 the following year. Why? Because due to inflation, the average price of a basket of goods has increased by 2-3%. Therefore, your money isn't as valuable as it was a year ago.

Put another way, imagine you spend $100 on groceries each week. If inflation is 2% per year, next year, those same groceries will cost $102. In 10 years, they'll cost about $122. That's the power of inflation: even if the number of groceries you're buying stays the same, the price goes up.

Over time, inflation reduces the value of cash sitting idle in a bank account. Therefore, the logical thing to do is invest.

"In a capitalist society, those without capital tend not to have power. I want to focus on liberating my community by giving them the knowledge and exposure to gain wealth."
Ross Mac

"We all
aspire to
be rich,
but are you
willing to

do what
it takes?
It takes
discipline."
Ross Mac

Chapter Five

The Best Kept Secret: Understanding the Stock Market

Now that we know why we need to invest, let's talk about how it fits into your financial freedom goals and how to go about it. Investing allows you to put your money into assets that have the potential to earn strong returns, outpacing inflation. And if done wisely, investing in the stock market can yield a much higher return compared to traditional banks. But what are stocks?

A stock is a security that represents fractional ownership in a company. When you buy a company's stock, you're purchasing a small piece of that company, called a share, making you a shareholder. As a shareholder, you have the right to share in the company's profitability, which can be distributed as dividends or reinvested back into the company. The value of these shares fluctuates based on a number of factors including the company's performance, economic conditions, and market sentiment. While investing in the stock market carries risk, it also provides the potential for substantial returns.

> "In investing, what is comfortable is rarely profitable."
> **Robert Arnott**

It's crucial to understand that investing should be viewed as a long-term strategy. While the stock market can be unpredictable in the short term, historically, it has trended upwards over the long term. If you look at all historical recessions, the stock market's value declined, however, in each case, it went on to recover and make new highs. Investing in the stock market is a lot more simple than you think.

When it comes to investing wisdom, few carry the authority of Warren Buffett, the legendary investor and chairman of Berkshire Hathaway. Known as the "Oracle of Omaha," Buffett has consistently advocated a simple, long-term approach to investing for small investors.

Buffett's advice to small investors has been quite straightforward: invest in S&P 500 index funds. The S&P 500 is a stock market index that includes 500 of the largest companies listed on the U.S. stock exchanges. By investing in an S&P 500 index fund, you're effectively investing in 500 different companies, providing instant diversification and reducing your risk compared to investing in individual stocks.

S&P 500 index funds typically have low expense ratios, meaning the cost to invest is minimal, which maximizes your return over the long run. In fact, over the long run, the S&P 500 has delivered an average annual return of around 10%, although this can vary year to year.

The strategy for investing in the S&P 500 is rather than trying to beat the stock market, which very few professionals can actually do, you passively invest in America's top performing companies across all different industries. This is a key to building wealth. You don't need to be a rocket scientist or psychic to learn from history. Over the long run, the stock market goes higher.

Wealth creation is a marathon, not a sprint. The journey involves making informed decisions, taking calculated risks, and above all, exercising patience. Starting to invest is a significant step on this journey. Remember, the goal is not to save money, but to grow it.

"In society, we're taught to be consumers, rather than to become owners. Something special happens when you feel ownership. The stock market turns you from a spectator to a player in the wealth game."
Ross Mac

Chapter Six

Building Block of Wealth: Investing in the Stock Market

So far, we've discussed the importance of investing, the wisdom of renowned investor Warren Buffett, the detrimental impact of inflation, and the basics of what stocks are. But, how does one begin to invest in the stock market? Let's break it down into a few straightforward steps:

Step 1: Set Clear Financial Goals

Before you invest, it's crucial to understand your financial goals. Are you investing for long-term goals like retirement or a child's education? Or are you aiming for short-term goals, such as a house down-payment in a few years? Knowing your time horizon and your risk tolerance helps guide your investment strategy.

Step 2: Create an Investment Budget

This brings us back to our first step. You have to decide how much money you can afford to invest. A common piece of advice is never to invest money that you can't afford to lose. It's generally wise to ensure you have a solid emergency fund and minimal high-interest debt before you begin investing. Why? Well because the average interest rate you pay on a credit card is over 20% and the average return in the stock market is roughly 10%. Therefore it makes more sense to use that extra money that you would

> "Our favorite holding period is forever."
> **Warren Buffett**

have invested to get out of debt sooner. Think about it! You are losing 20% to make 10%. That math isn't good!

Step 3: Open an Investment Account

To start investing in stocks, you'll need an investment account. For most people, this means opening a brokerage account. A brokerage account allows you to buy and sell investments, including stocks. Over the years, online brokerages have democratized access to the stock market and generally have lower fees than traditional brokerages. A few examples of brokerage firms are Etrade, Robinhood, Fidelity, and Sofi to name a few.

Step 4: Understand Diversification

Diversification involves spreading your investments across various types of assets (such as stocks, bonds, and real estate) to reduce risk. One way to diversify when investing in stocks is to invest in different sectors or industries, like technology, healthcare, or consumer goods. For instance, if you were to only own airline companies during March of 2020, when Covid-19 hit, your portfolio would have been down over 50%. Being diversified helps minimize the risk of one event materially impacting your portfolio.

Step 5: Choose Your Investments

Following Warren Buffett's advice, an S&P 500 index is where you start. It offers instant diversification across several sectors and companies. However, depending on your risk tolerance and financial goals, you may also wish to invest in individual stocks, other types of funds (like sector or industry funds), bonds, or even real estate investment trusts (REITs).

We are taught to pay bills monthly. But now, let's pay ourselves monthly as well. You need to set up auto-investing so that you can take the guessing work out of investing. The goal is to invest a few hundred dollars monthly and look back in 30 years with over one million dollars to retire with. Sure the market will fluctuate, but investing monthly allows you to dollar cost average. This means you are buying the same assets at a regular interval, regardless of the price.

Successful investing typically involves a long-term approach. Despite the occasional market downturn, the stock market has historically trended upward over the long term. As Warren Buffett famously said, "Our favorite holding period is forever."

Investing in the stock market is a critical step in your journey towards financial freedom and generational wealth. By understanding how the stock market works and following these steps, you can leverage investing as a powerful tool for wealth accumulation. Remember, the earlier you start investing, the more time your money has to grow due to compound interest.

Compound interest is "interest on interest." In other words, it's the interest that is calculated on the initial investment, and that interest is reinvested, thus making interest on the reinvested interest. The compound effect is how wealth is grown.

> "Retire from work, but not from life."
> **M.K. Soni**

Chapter Seven

Your Golden Years: Investing for Retirement

I n our journey towards financial freedom and generational wealth, one crucial stop is planning for retirement. The goal isn't just to retire comfortably, but to retire with the financial freedom to do what you love, when you want, without worrying about money. So let's talk about retirement investment strategies, particularly through 401(k) plans and Roth IRAs.

Retirement investment accounts like 401(k)s and Roth IRAs offer unique tax advantages that can greatly enhance your wealth accumulation over time.

A 401(k) is a retirement savings plan offered by many employers. It allows employees to save and invest a portion of their paycheck before taxes are taken out. In this plan, employees can contribute $22,500 for individuals under 50 and $30,000 for those 50 and older (as of 2023 tax code).

401(k) plans are tax deferred, meaning, you set aside part of your pay before federal and state income taxes are withheld, lowering your taxable income so you pay less income tax now. With a tax-deferred 401(k), you don't pay taxes on the earnings as you make them every year.

The IRS lets you begin to withdraw without a penalty at age 591/2. When you withdraw, you pay taxes

> "Fortune sides with him who dares."
> **Virgil**

at your current tax rate. It's important to note, your taxable income often drops in retirement, potentially putting you into a lower tax bracket than you had as an employee. If for some reason you need to withdraw money early, you will usually pay taxes plus a 10% early withdrawal penalty.

The key with 401(k) plans is employer match programs. This is when employers offer to match your 401(k) contributions up to a certain percentage of your salary. This is essentially free money that can significantly increase your retirement savings. As a rule of thumb, always aim to contribute at least enough to get the full employer match. Make sure you get your free money!

Not everyone works for a company or for a company that offers 401(k) plans. For those individuals, they should open a Roth IRA. A Roth IRA is an individual retirement account that offers tax-free growth and tax-free withdrawals in retirement, as long as certain conditions are met.

Roth IRA contributions are made with after-tax dollars, therefore, your money grows tax-free and you won't have to pay taxes on withdrawals in retirement. This can be particularly advantageous if you expect to be in a higher tax bracket in retirement than you are now. Another thing to consider, you have no idea what the tax code will look like when you reach retirement age. It can always be much higher than it is now.

As of 2023, the maximum contribution to a Roth IRA is $6,500 per year, or $7,500 if you're age 50 or older.

If you don't have access to a 401(k), opening a Roth IRA is a great alternative. Even if you do have a 401(k), you might consider contributing to a Roth IRA as well to diversify your retirement savings.

Investing for retirement is essential for several reasons. For one, life expectancy is continuously increasing so you'll need more money to sustain a longer retirement. Another thing to consider is inflation. The cost of living will continue to increase, as well healthcare costs.

It's understandable that the concept of retirement might seem far away, but it should be a priority. The decisions you make today will significantly influence your financial stability in your later years. By investing wisely and taking advantage of retirement savings accounts like 401(k)s and Roth IRAs, you can build a nest egg that will allow you to enjoy your golden years in comfort and financial security.

Basic financial concepts

Compound Interest: The power of compound interest makes saving for retirement extremely effective. The sooner you start, the more time your money has to grow.

Tax Advantages: Retirement accounts like 401(k)s and Roth IRAs offer substantial tax benefits. Contributions to a 401(k) lower your taxable income, while Roth IRA withdrawals are tax-free in retirement.

Employer Contributions: If your employer offers a 401(k) match, take full advantage. It's essentially free money contributing towards your future financial freedom.

Author's Note

Planting Seeds for the Next Generation: Securing Your Children's Future

Building generational wealth isn't just about achieving personal financial freedom; it's about creating a financial legacy for your children and setting them up for success. It's important to focus on strategies to secure your children's financial future, which can be achieved through life insurance, custodial accounts, and 529 plans.

We aren't going to live forever. Now that we understand that, preparing for that unfortunate but certain circumstance can be the difference in how your family mourns. It's bad enough that a loved one is passing away, but imagine you leaving your family on the hook for your debts and/or funeral costs. If your death would financially impact the people in your life, then you need life insurance.

Life insurance is a contract between you and an insurance company. You make regular payments (premiums), and in exchange, the insurance company pays a lump sum (death benefit) to your beneficiaries when you pass away. Life insurance provides a financial safety net for your family. If something were to happen to you, the death benefit could help cover daily living expenses, pay off debts, fund your child's education, or even act as an inheritance.

How much life insurance do you need? A general rule of thumb is to have roughly 10x your annual salary. So for instance, if you make $80,000 per year, then you should get a $800,000 life insurance policy. Life insurance is meant to replace your income for your loved ones when you pass away.

The 2 most common forms of life insurance are Terms vs. Whole Life Insurance. Term life insurance provides coverage for a certain period, usually 10, 20, or 30 years, and is generally less expensive. Whole life insurance provides coverage for your entire life and has a cash value component that can be borrowed against. There are pros and cons to both forms, but at a minimum, a person should start with at least term life insurance.

Many parents realize that to give their kids the best chance of financial success, they need to set aside some time to teach their kids fiscal responsibility and set aside money. A custodial account for minors can be a tool that accomplishes both.

A custodial account is a savings account at a financial institution, mutual fund company, or brokerage firm that adults control for minors. The two main types are the Uniform Transfers to Minors Act (UTMA) and the Uniform Gifts to Minors Act (UGMA).

These accounts allow you to invest in stocks, bonds, mutual funds, and other assets on behalf of a minor. This can potentially lead to significant growth over time. The investments in custodial accounts become the property of the minor when they reach the age of 18, giving them a financial head start in adulthood. Along the way, these accounts can help teach your children how to become owners of the companies that they are customers of. If your child wears Nikes, eats McDonald's and is on YouTube all day, might as well teach them how to own those companies as well.

The last thought to consider is giving your kids the ability to not incur student loans. That's where a 529 account comes in.

A 529 plan is a tax-advantaged savings plan designed to encourage saving for future education costs. These can be used for college expenses and, up to a certain amount, for private K-12 education. It allows you to save money for your child's education and grows tax-free. Withdrawals for qualifying education expenses are also tax-free. In fact, many states offer tax deductions or credits for contributions to a 529 plan.

It's crucial to start planning for your child's financial future as early as possible. Life insurance, custodial accounts, and 529 plans are all important tools that can be used to build a financial safety net and provide opportunities for your children.

Remember, the goal of building generational wealth is not just to improve your life, but also to provide a solid financial foundation for your children and future generations. In the vast tapestry of life, the thread of financial security is a defining element, woven into every stage and aspect of our existence. Cultivating generational wealth is not merely about accumulating money; it's about forging a legacy, cementing a secure future for ourselves and the generations that follow.

The concept goes beyond individual prosperity, extending to the well-being of our families, communities, and ultimately, society at large. It is about creating opportunities, ensuring comfort, and most importantly, securing freedom; the freedom to make choices, to navigate life's challenges, and to realize our dreams.

Remember, the actions we take today cast long shadows into the future. A financially free tomorrow begins with being intentional and informed today. So, let's begin this journey. Let's weave our tapestry with threads of financial wisdom and commitment. Because a future of financial freedom isn't just a dream; it's a decision, a process, and finally, a reality.

Ross Mac

"Once we start becoming financially free

we can hopefully become politically free."

Ross Mac

Made in the USA
Middletown, DE
29 August 2024

60008007R00029